Peter Williams

Values
Based Education

**Practical Strategies
To Start, Strengthen and Sustain
Values Based Learning**

Author: Peter Williams

Title: VALUES - BASED EDUCATION
Practical Strategies To Start, Strengthen and Sustain Values
Based Learning

First Edition: 2019

© 2019 Peter Williams
ISBN: 9781796633603

peter.williams@livingvalues.net

CONTENTS

End Piece

Part 1

Overview

The K-12 Kuwait American School was founded on the Living Values Education Program in 1999. After 20 continuous years of implementing Living Values Education, its vision and mission continue to 'Build Minds, Characters and Futures' within an international context of 'Learning without Borders'.

Setting the Context

Setting the context addresses 4 key questions:

i. How and why was a Living Values-based school created?

ii. After 20 years, what three key principles did we learn along the way?

iii. What are some of the evidence indicating the benefits of Living Values Education?

iv. What preparations did the Founding Principal have to put in place?

How and why was a Living Values Education school created?

In 1999, Kuwait had suffered from an invasion and the Founder's vision, Mrs. Wajeeha Al-Habib, was to help heal the peacelessness in the hearts and minds of adults and children in Kuwait by creating a values-based school. She witnessed that children of all ages had become traumatized and, even though many said her vision would not work - her determination - with Living Values Education and a team of like-minded educators made it possible.

Ask any parent what they wish for their child and most will say 'Peace and Happiness' and ask any parent what value or quality they would like their child to carry with them all of their lives and most will say 'Honesty'. It was with this understanding that Living Values Education set the foundation for the school with hope, trust and a secure vision with values at its heart. The school believed that in every child there was a seed waiting to bloom. The metaphor of a star and a diamond helps to illustrate this practical vision with the star representing the child's innate gifts and skills and the diamond representing all their values that shine from the heart.

In addition to delivering a Council for International Schools accredited and rigorous academic curriculum, the Living Values Education with its vision, creativity, clarity, guidance, and practicalities has enabled the school to identify and nurture three key principles.

After 20 years, what three key principles did the school learn along the way?

1. The Loving Presence of the Educator in a Values-Based Atmosphere who models and lives their values with Kindness

The presence of the educator who modeled and lived their values with kindness was a key message. Whilst accepting that we are all working on how to live our most positive values, we discovered that the children were modeling themselves on us and learning to appreciate that a values-based atmosphere based on love, values, respect, understanding, and safety generated a positive energy and willingness to learn with trust in their ability, clarity, safety and kindness.

2. The Importance of Enabling a Community of Trust and a Family of Learners, especially with parents, in the promotion of well-being, care and high quality learning for their children

Parents were surveyed as to what made the school a place where they could send their child 'to learn', 'to belong' and 'to be' themselves. Their top 5 responses were: A place where you feel welcomed, a place to feel at ease with yourself, a place to know yourself, a place to feel part of a family and a place to feel loved, valued, respected, understood and safe. It is interesting to note that no parent mentioned academics.

3. The confidence and trust that there is Healing Strength in nurturing and guiding hearts and minds through Living Values Education

What began in 1999 with some hurt and violence amongst some traumatized students soon, with the help of Living Values Education, turned into laughter, joy, happiness and learning in both the head and heart. In 2007, the school carried out a survey with the senior students with regard to their reflections, wishes, and hopes. There were many positive responses including the ability to make ethical choices, yet, one response was unexpected. The students felt that blame and shame were still too much in evidence and affecting their lives. When the school asked what the school was doing to cause blame and shame, the students responded that it wasn't the school causing blame and shame, but adults of the world who, they felt, need to stop blaming and shaming others and must start forgiving, forgetting, trusting and moving on.

We began to wonder – could Living Values Education truly help to build a better world? The students said 'Yes'.

What is the evidence indicating the benefits of Living Values Education?

- The school has grown to be a family – a community of learners.
- There is a powerful values-based learning atmosphere.
- There is a strong feeling of welcome, joy, and accep-

tance.
- The students express their values using their own moral compass.
- The students became ambassadors of how to live their values.
- There are very few referrals for physical violence.
- Peace Time and Mindfulness is widely practiced.
- The academic standards are higher.
- The school's assemblies provide an essential focus for the Living Value of the Month led by students and staff.
- Lead assemblies, once per month, are in Arabic and English to help assure relevance in cultural context.
- Living Values Education lessons are supported by unique Etiquette, Public Speaking, and Life Skills programs that are 'taught' each week.
- Values-based learning is being incorporated, where applicable, into the Middle and High School years.
- For educators, it's a great place to come to work each day to give of your best with a result that teaching is enjoyable. Staff retention levels are very high, and
- For everyone, the school is a happy and hardworking place to be.

A recent visitor from the Ministry of Youth commented: 'Why are these students so happy and learning so well? We responded: 'It's a Living Values School'.

What professional competencies, adjustments, and personal attributes did the leader of a brand new values-based school put into place and sustain?

For Personal Preparation

• Take the best of my knowledge, skills, and experience that I had learnt within the context I had been a professional for 30 years and start again.

• Listen, watch and ask.

• Adapt to a new cultural interpretation of values with a universal values heart.

• Remember that I was a guest in another country to learn and to share.

• Set the vision, not by imposition, but by invitation to join the mission.

• Nurture from the root and wait for the flower to bloom with patience.

• Go slowly with no quick fixes expected.

For School Preparation

• Place the desired value(s) ahead of all that the school was seeking to achieve in all areas of teaching, learning and administration followed by the subject matter and how to deliver it.

• Assure that the legal curriculum guidelines and expectations were met.

• To train all educators with regard to Living Values Education at the start of each academic year.

• To set transparent strategic short, medium and long-term plans – leading the school from the original concept of a K-5 living values-based school to a K-12 fully accredited living values-based school.

• To see the very best in every child, of all ages, and to envision them better than they believe themselves to be.

• To lead Living Values assemblies each week with exemplars of how the staff and students may wish to take part and take the lead.

• Appreciate that the goodness of Living Values genuinely attracts the right people to its presence.

• Communicate widely with parents including the facilitation of workshops.

To Raise the School's and Living Values Education profile

• Attend the Education for All conference in Cairo to share the benefits of Living Values Education, and afterwards, at the invitation of UNESCO, to co-address all Arab Ministers of Education in Beirut.

• Inform, by Ministerial invitation, all 800 Kuwait State Schools about the benefits of the Living Values Education Program.

• Apply and gain approval for the school to be an approved Ministry of Education Living Values Training School.

• Offer regular In-Service Training Living Values workshops and seminars in Kuwait to interested schools, Universities and NGO's.

- Take 'Living Values' into the community by way of values-based theatrical productions, for example, The Little Prince and Jonathan Seagull.
- Train, facilitate, listen and learn in neighboring countries eg Saudi Arabia, Oman, Dubai, Egypt.

Safety for All

- Working in a conflict zone – assure the physical safety for all both within and outside the school with protocols securely in place.
- Reminding myself that some colleagues had witnessed and were affected by the traumas of economic challenges and war.......and continue to be affected to this day.
- Securely inform a safe learning and empowering growth environment for all with no 'put downs' for colleagues who were navigating this approach for the first time.
- To firmly establish and maintain a positive atmosphere of love, care, and kindness with an occasional lawful reminder!

To Value, Nurture and Train the Educator

- Employ and build a team of like-minded values-based educators.
- Appreciate the staff 100% with an unswerving commitment to their welfare and responsibility.
- Trust my colleagues 100% knowing that no-one was perfect especially myself.

• Fully nurture and actively support the warm-hearted and caring educator.
• Empower and encourage best practices and sharing the same.
• To invite and train educators to be Living Values Trainers/ Facilitators. (This carried significant benefit for the students and the school's growth.)

When things became challenging

• Learn to manage criticism from 'traditional assessors' where their given remit was not to assess soft skills.
• Be calm in times of paradox, multiple expectations and be prepared to step right outside of your comfort zone.
• Be prepared to embrace change, the unexpected and unpredictability.
• Have unswerving faith, sometimes against all odds, that this form of learning is successful.
• To gently guide and nurture everyone.
• Accept and show my own vulnerability.
• Learn to take 'time out' for the self.

Keep nurturing the seed with servant leadership

• To emerge and develop servant leadership with kindness and resilience.
• Support the Living Values root and take care of the many shoots!
• Lead and fill the gaps when things are forgotten. You only have to do it once with no criticism given.

• To keep the vision alive and 'clean' with regular training and 'reminders' at the start of each academic year, especially for new to school teachers.
• Nourish, understand and appreciate that people are affected by the respect we share with them regardless of gender, faith or nationality.
• Be open to adopting other values-based approaches that awaken and nurture values.
• To be always available with 'no door' to my office area.

Above all:

• Be the Example and be the Model.
• Create a Loving Presence.
• Enable a Community of Trust
• Nurture the Healing strength of Living Values Education
• Educate from the Heart.
• Know myself and how I live my values.
• Always plan for succession.
• Be thankful.

The journey was supported by many practical steps that support the three principles. They can be introduced according to local circumstance and preference.

Part 2

30 Practical Strategies that added to the school's Living Values Education vision

Each practical strategy carries an equality of contribution with strategies 1, 2 and 3 essential to secure the foundation.

Once strategies 1, 2 and 3 are secure, <u>consider choosing one or two to focus on</u> from the strategies below according to culture and context.

Take your time. Living Values and all values-based approaches to learning cannot be rushed or 'done overnight'. Be patient and take rest from time to time.

The KAS model, with a school population of 650+ representing 30+ nationalities, took 10 years to embed and we are still learning and adapting.

The Three Essentials

1. Inviting everyone to contribute to the Values and Vision

Key Message: Living Values is not a 'top-down' model. It's an empowering model for all from the root.

Inviting everyone to visualize what the school should look and feel like, in words and images, assisted in exploring ways in which everyone can reflect on how their own practice, gifts, and talents can add to the vision.

Key to the success of this approach is that the vision is not 'top-down' but an equality of contribution towards one agreed vision to which teachers, leaders, management and the whole school community can play their part.

It is essential that the process is nurtured and natural 'from the root' and not forced or controlled 'from above'. Force or control is a dictate and can wound the spirit of the educator. Nurturing invites in and allows each one of us to bring our emotional and spiritual self to our role and profession.

Suggestion: Invite everyone, in a group setting, to share and record what values are important to them in education.
Trust and value all responses. This is the shared vision.

2. Creating the Atmosphere

Key Message: *Keep positive – no matter what!*

Positive atmospheres invite LVRUS – love, values, respect, understanding, and security to the learner and educator. Laws apply yet the lawmaking within a positive atmosphere is to be lawful to oneself and the cultural norms in which one lives and learns. The love in positive atmospheres is to give love, respect, regard and bring one's naturalness in the situation. Positive atmospheres uplift independence in learning, assure love for learning and assure success that is sustainable over time. Positive atmospheres nurture well-being as well as academic growth.

Suggestion: *Personally welcome everyone, with a smile and a kind word, at the start of the school day – colleagues as they enter the building and students as they enter the gate.*

3. Character Education with the depth of Living Values Education

Key Message: *The education of character and living values is the foundation*

This lies at the heart of a Living Values School. It is for everyone. Using the Living Values Education materials, it is practiced each day and touches the heart of the child and educator by:

- Inviting their presence, their voice, their experience, and contribution
- Honoring cultural roots, traditions, and goodness
- Understanding their circumstances and lifestyle
- Inviting the knowing heart to bring to fruition a positive difference
- Giving permission to help co-create a better world.

The essence of Living Values is to invite and to work with or alongside others with shared values from the heart. It is certainly not a program to be 'filled into others' rather than a 'drawing out' of what is already there.

Suggestion: *Explore, experience and express the Living Values materials every day. Most of all - Enjoy the journey!*

After the essentials, choose one or two from the following strategies to focus on according to your culture and context and then continue to explore, experience and express other strategies in your own time managed way.

4. Celebrating Good Practice in the Classroom and Around School

Key Message: *Catch everyone doing things right and appreciate.*

Celebrating the good practice that is already there builds appreciative trust and capacity for growth to which each school will rightly find its own way to acknowledge according to their own conventions and protocols. An 'easy does it' and 'gentle steps' approach – leading by example, celebrating our current strengths, catching everyone 'doing things right' and celebrating the many steps along the way, I believe, helps to build and uplift the spirit and values-based application of learning. For example, gently instilling the application of appreciative inquiry with 'no put-downs' yet 'raising the bar' to become even better at doing your best.

Suggestion: *Enter classes and offer a specifically focused positive affirmation.*

5. The important role of Assemblies

Key Message: *Living Values assemblies create a sense of family and modeled unity. Cultural stories and 'mother tongue assemblies' are a regular feature.*

Living Values-based assemblies are a very positive way to create a sense of family, togetherness and modeled unity. They help the school to envision and maintain its values and how to live them in a practical way.

The 12 key Living Values Education materials, as explored, experienced and expressed in the classroom and around school form the basis all assemblies. The key elements in most assemblies include: stillness, a song, story, play, and reflection. Parents are regularly invited to attend.

The importance of sharing stories and cultural values in the mother tongue of the children, followed by an English interpretation, is often used to add towards the making of a unity of values for all. These values are illustrated and displayed around the school at the children's eye level.

Suggestion: *Place children's work and posters around the school highlighting the values(s) of the month with a message.*

6. Etiquette and Social Acceptability

Key Message: *Learn to look after yourself and to be a lovely person to know in whatever culture, circumstance or context you find yourself.*

Etiquette

Taught as a foundation lesson alongside Living Values Education, Etiquette instills principles of common courtesy and consideration for others with regard to comfort, respect, taste, feeling and privacy. In a nutshell: 'Do to others what you would like to have happen to you'.

Examples of the 30 step program include: How to greet one another, Introductions in a number of contexts, How to say 'please' and 'thank you', How to answer a phone, How to open and close a conversation, Table Manners, Personal Hygiene and Public Speaking.

Public Speaking

Public Speaking is an art that requires training and confidence building to be fully prepared for whatever values-based context the student will find themselves in the future.

Avenues to explore, experience and express include:

- Show and Tell – bringing an item or book from home to share.
- Interviews – teacher to student, student to student, student to a guest speaker.
- Front of Camera – preparing a speech and speaking to the camera.
- Role Play – confidence in acting.
- Open Sharing.

Adding value to voice and confidence in presenting the message can be 'measured', over time, using a number of indicators:

- Has confidence
- Shows enthusiasm toward public speaking
- Speaks clearly. Uses inflection in tone
- Speaks slowly, annunciating every word
- Has a stable body posture.
- Is respectful of all – no matter what!

In an age where the loss of dialogue in favor of texting or messaging is becoming more prevalent, perhaps the enhancement of public speaking programs are a way to help empower students with the entrepreneurial and communication skills necessary to be successful where it really matters.

Suggestion: Consider inviting the children to create their own 'Etiquette Code of Conduct' – one for school and one for home – and talk about it to the camera with a voice full of values.

7. Your Voice is the first Musical Instrument

Key Message: The voice is the first musical instrument.
The voice reflects the sound of the human soul where tonality and inflection carry the values between the words.

Our voice helps to uplift the values-based spirit of learning:

- To instruct, explore, inspire and connect
- To soften, to focus, to strengthen and to relax
- To call, to resonate with our own true self and to touch the soul
- To celebrate our message.

No need to shout!

Music, in all its forms, is also the alchemy of sound that touches the heart and soul in us all. The music shifts consciousness with a 'felt shift' that is forgotten in its presence.

For example:

- Music played at lower beats enhances creativity
- Music played at 60 beats per minute is ideal for learning Mathematics
- Softly played music reduces stress and soothes the tired mind
- Rousing music creates a feeling of action and pride
- Music brings harmony with the self and others.

Music and the Music of the Voice helps to soften the resistance to move on.

Suggestion: Let the music of your voice mean more than the words that are spoken.

8. Your Presence is a Living Art Form

Key Message: Our very presence is a living Art Form. How we 'carry' ourselves is on show all the time.

The comfort and security that we, as educators, give to a child is priceless. Whether we are silent, use sound and silence or sound – our presence is on show all the time. We are each a living Art form of how we live our values. Our altruism cannot be hidden. At its best it is warm-heartedness.

Suggestion: Your presence is a Living Art form that speaks through presence and silence. Live well and be kind to yourself. It shows and is felt.

9. The Value of Luminosity

Key Message: *When children are learning with a feeling of being loved, valued, respected, understood and safe, their faces glow. This luminosity is tangible, felt and leads to successful achievement in the heart, mind, soul, and academics.*

Love of learning brings a brightness of heart with a genuine, authentic and honest pursuit of knowledge and giving that lightens up our DNA and neural pathways. This brightness of heart simply adds luminosity to the faces and eyes of all students, and uplifts their learning potential through, amongst others:

- Appreciating one's presence and one's contribution however big or small
- Showing positive regard for others with the language of the eyes and a warm smile to uplift and encourage
- Engendering a warm sense of belonging and togetherness
- Sharing the joy of success with no put-downs
- Giving a listening ear to encourage and acknowledge
- Being true to oneself with the moral courage to do what is right

Suggestion: *Nurture positive regard in all its forms to add brightness to the heart of learning*

10. Create and Aim - Imagine Achievement in Life

Key Message: *Do we each have an aim in life?*

Many children, of all ages, don't have an aim in life. Sports people and Olympic stars imagine achievement in their life and make it happen. They visualize their success. In these terms, as you hold the vision, that is what you receive.

To help in the process, consider the stages of learning as researched by Richard Barrett.

- A baby aged 0 to 2 years needs love, comfort, and basic needs
- A child aged 3 to 11 years needs to feel loved, valued, respected, understood and safe
- A young adult ages 11 to 15 years needs to be recognized for their achievements
- A young adult aged 15 to 18 years seeks purpose
- A young adult aged 18 to 35 years seeks security, employment, and succession
- A mature adult ages 35 to 45 years seeks meaning to life, and
- A retired person returns to wishing to feel loved, valued, respected, understood and secure.

Putting it simply, whatever your age or age of the children, visualize and ignite the spirit within and wait for the flower to bloom in its own time. Lock the spirit within to fixed learning with a fixed time frame and the flower may bloom or it may fade away.

Suggestion: Take time out to create your aim then set out to make it happen.

11. Peace Time

Key Message: Give everyone in school the permission to slow down the hurried mind and do 'nothing'.

Peacetime is observed around 10 am each working day with the playing of soft instrumental music across the full schools' sound system. This Peace Time lasts for no longer than 2 minutes genuinely adding to the school day and learning about themselves rather than 'taking away teaching and learning time'.

Additional Peace Time activities include: silence generated by switching off the lights, playing soft instrumental music, gently stretching exercises, visualization, storytelling with reflective pauses and Tai Chi.

Suggestion: Give yourself an invitation to enjoy this 2-minute practice each day. It helps to re-charge, re-focus and keeps stress away.

12. Contemplation, Meditation and Creative Visualisation

Key Message: *Open doors to more than a 'one-way' values approach through guided contemplation, meditation, and creative visualization.*

Guided Contemplation

Guided contemplation is taking the children on a picture journey in their mind's eye. Every journey is different and every journey is just as it should be! No judgment is involved – just acceptance.

Meditation

Often defined as 'Mindfulness', meditation takes children to a safe, still and peaceful place. It helps to heal the wounded spirit and re-charge the batteries. Its benefits include: clarity, calmness, happiness, and sense of purpose.

Creative Visualisation

Creative visualisation is taking children on an inner journey – carefully guiding them through their thoughts – in a gentle and nonprescribed way. For example: What would the journey of a drop of water inside of a plant look like? After the visualization, talk about the journey. Accept all answers as correct. Invite the students to do a storyboard with 4, 6 or 8 pictures, a poem, or a creative story about the 'journey of a drop of water'. Enable the children, not yourself, to display them.

Relax Kids stories are particularly effective in bringing children into values-based 'guided contemplative and creative visualization spaces'.

The results include: increased self-respect, increased attentiveness, a safe place to be quiet, better social interaction, more kindness, more original and creative work especially with art and writing, and better standardized and nonverbal test scores.

Intuitive teachers just know when reflection is required and when doing is the order of the day. It's what professional teachers all over the world instinctively know what to do and how to do it. It is their gift to humanity.

Suggestion: Keep thinking 'out of the box'. Relax and 'Be' yourself. Your children and colleagues will love you even more for it and will enjoy joining in!

13. Journaling

Key Message: Journaling adds depth to learning a life of values.

Journaling is personal writing with time to do it. Journaling slows down the 'hurried child' away from tests and assessments into a celebration of their own thinking. It gives time to consider the 'big' and 'little' things in life and brings focus to learning. The contemplative quality of journaling awakens imagination, integrity and an 'inner conversation' that is sometimes denied.

Amongst other benefits, journaling as a regular practice:

• Invites children to reflect on their inner world with ways to show it on the outside.
• Helps them understand that we all think and 'see things' differently.
• Brings an awareness that behind every action in themselves and another person is a reservoir of previous experiences that shape their lives and the lives in others,

Suggestion: Consider this approach to help focus and take the hurried child away from distractions and overused social media.

14. Story Telling

Key Message: We all have a story to tell. This process helps us to appreciate and to listen.

Story Telling is the gateway to the vivid imagination of the inner world with a voice, the presence of one another and mountains of imagination. Stories take children on a journey into a world of fact, fantasy and fun. Some stories are best read out, some are best changed to culture and context, and some are best read with children's full participation in costume.

Story Tellers use a range of voice pitches, speed and modulation to capture the audience with a sense of wonder and, in doing so, touch an inner chord of truth in the child. Story Telling is also about telling events in our lives that we would like to share with others. One's presence and attentiveness to listen rather than hear adds to the true meaning of storytelling.

Suggestion: Encourage parents to read a story to their child/ children every night. Listen, too, to the life stories of children. 'Once upon a time' could take on a whole new meaning!

15. Drama and Psychodrama

Key Message: Some children and adults are locked into one way of thinking. Drama and Psychodrama awakens us to the traditional and 'hidden' mysteries in our lives.

Drama

Through drama, releasing expression, touching emotion and firing the imagination ignites the values-based heart in us all. How often do parents come and watch and photograph their children on stage during national festivities and special productions that retell events of long ago and celebrate the nation's identity? Acting out plays of stories, enchantment, fairy tales, myths, legends, and religious occasions also bring a pride to the spirit of giving.

Psychodrama

Psychodrama heals and shows mastery of its effect through the giving of a message. For example, inviting the children, usually in assembly, to witness a journey of good over bad with good humor. Imagine the scene where 2 actors are acting out good v not so good eating habits. One actor eats healthy food and another actor eats only junk food. The children laugh when they see the two characters. Afterwards, they are asked which is better – healthy eating or unhealthy eating? Without exception, they always choose healthy food, whilst being honest enough to admit that they do both!

Suggestion: Create a stage and let the children take the lead.

16. Kelso's Choices – A conflict resolution tool

Key Message: Empower children to make their own values-based choices

Kelso's Choices Resolution program is a complementary and successful tool to help very young to aged 9 children to manage their own conflicts and problems with the assistance of a puppet frog who brings problem-solving choices. The program helps the students to identify the difference between 'big' problems like getting hurt, feeling scared, being bullied and the importance of telling a trusted adult straight away – and 'small' problems.

Bright posters are posted around the school with 2 key messages:

a. If you have a big problem – tell an adult you trust.
b. If you have a small problem – try 2 of Kelso's choices

namely:

- talk it out
- share and take turns
- ignore it
- walk away
- tell them to stop
- apologise
- make a deal
- wait and cool off
- go to another game.

Suggestion: In assemblies, make it OK to tell about 'big problems' – and to work out your own 'little ones'. Consider inviting the older children to co-lead the assembly.

17. Philosophy and Working with Words and Quotations

i. Philosophy

Key Message: Philosophy is for all.
It's root meaning, in Greek, is: 'Love of Wisdom'.

Pondering the awe, wonder and paradoxes of life captivate the imagination and inner world of children. Lipman's pioneering Philosophy for Children (P4C) uses stories to bring children to the point of choice – choice in the decision making and knowing which choice is the right one for them.

Equally, some paradoxes are unanswerable creating space for creativity, future possibilities and imagination to flourish. For example: Is life a stage on which we all play our part? What is infinity? If you go through a black hole, what is on the other side? Is there such a thing as an enchantment? Are fairy stories real?

Philosophy invites in the twists, turns and a never-ending story.

Suggestion: *In very young children, there is an innocence and an unbridled voice of simplistic wisdom. Ask them the hardest questions. They will, for sure, give you the answer!*

ii. Working with Quotations and Words

Key Message: *Ancient Wisdom and Quotations carry many messages for Modern Times.*

Quotations abound and each carries a different message to the receiver. Inviting students to discover and discuss quotations is a lively way to articulate points of view, respect others point of view and build both respect and self-respect.

Only 600 out of 6000 languages are secure and strengthen the call for upholding the meanings, traditions, and values of individual languages. The emergence of bi-lingualism of values creates structured spaces to discuss points of common interest, appreciates differences, enhances the well-being of individuals and society and generates a constant flow of affirmative messages. Assemblies using multiple languages helps to keep these traditions alive. For example: What does peace mean to you?

Suggestion: Seek an Ancient Wisdom quote and bring its meaning into your life. It may be, or may not be, the same interpretation as your best friend!

18. Linking Art with Literature and Healing

Key Message: Art invites the heart to express where words cannot. Art has no borders. It's a silent alchemy.

Art and Literature

Imagine a Grade 1/ Year 1 Art Class of bright-eyed children sitting in a circle listening to the story of the Princess and the Pea. You will recall that to be a pure-hearted Princess, the girl had to know if a pea was underneath 20 mattresses that she was resting on. Imagine the story being shared to the children with the 'formal objectives' of the lesson being to draw lines in different thicknesses, forms, and expressions. Imagine now the student's face as they drew 20 lines of their own choosing to represent the mattresses with a picture of the princess on the top and the pea on the bottom! All learning objectives were met in a fun way with a story to share with mums and dads when the children went home.

Art offers a Healing Property

Children affected by trauma or war have a yearning to express their feelings where words are not enough. For example: students from one war affected land drew pictures for students in another war affected land. The pictures offered peace and hope and were exhibited in both lands. They drew a silent knowing from all those who witnessed their images – not one of conflict – but only hope and peace.

Other ways of joint activities between the two countries include:

a. Starting a picture in one country and asking students in a twin school to complete it.

b. Writing a story between two nations/ two cultures.

c. Take part in a Joint Sustainable Futures project.

Suggestion: Appreciate Art and the numerous perspectives that invite the artist in each one of us to explore, experience and express. Love and appreciate your own living your values Art form.

19. Nature and Outdoor Education

Key Message: We are part of Nature. It's our Mother Earth home.

Children feel natural and at ease in the outdoors. Just watch them play. They learn more about themselves and personality in the outdoors than the protected four walls of the classroom. Children are drawn to nature and nature helps them to identify who they are.

For example: Beach sculpture excites children. Imagine collecting natural items on a beach and creating collage or mural on the sand. Working in teams, each child will contribute to a different perspective. Sharing, caring and contributing to the picture is a team effort. It's enjoyed and then swept away by the tide.

Now imagine two egotistical youngsters who were put together for an orienteering course. One could read a map and not a compass and the other could use a compass but not read a map. Without co-operation, they would not have succeeded in the task. They learnt to put egos to one side and co-operate. They learnt humility. Similarly, two non-communicative children were put into a two-man canoe to paddle downstream. If you paddle on one side only, the boat goes around in circles! Communicate and the canoe goes in a straight line. The children learnt to communicate.

Mother Nature is stronger than we are as humans and sometimes we forget to honor it. Working in, about and for nature has never been as vital as it is today.

Suggestion: Play and learn more outside in nature.

20. Stilling Techniques, 'Time for Me' and the Benefits of Silence

Key Message: Remember to be a 'Human Being' - not just a 'Human Doing'.

Being in nature, stilling, silence and 'time for me' are great friends to us all and take us away from the hurried world of 'doing' to help reflect, consider the direction we wish to take and most importantly, book an appointment with our self!

According to UNESCO's – Learning: The Treasure Within – there are four components: Learning to Know, Learning to Do, Learning to Belong and Learning to Be.

Almost 20 years after the report was published, the Head of UNESCO shared: 'We have become very good at knowing and doing, but we have forgotten how to belong with one another in peace and harmony and simply be a 'human being' rather than a 'human doing'.

This is where the part of being in nature, stilling, silence and 'time for me' enables each of us to access and reflect on our inner world and values in our own unique way.

Suggestion: Make 'stilling' time an approved practice from which everyone can benefit.

21. Preferred types of learning for Introverts and Extroverts

Key message: We all learn differently and cooperation is the key

Is it true that educators prefer speedy 'hands up' class responses that encourage the extrovert to share more quickly than the quiet introvert?

At the Kuwait American School in October 2017, 34 educators - of which there were 23 introverts and 11 extroverts - put this claim to the test by taking part in a professional development day that addressed four different learning approaches. The four modeled approaches were

- Quiet Reflection Time
- Partner Talk e.g. think: pair: share
- Table Talk
- Presenter Talk

At the end of the day, each individual's favorite type of learning was shared by way of a confidential 'exit poll'.

It was anticipated that the introverts would pick mainly reflection time. Not true. 65% of the introverts chose 'table talk' helping us to understand the fundamental role cooperation plays in learning.

The results were:

Quiet Reflection Time: Total 5 (0 extroverts and 5 introverts).

Partner Talk: Total 5 (2 extroverts and 3 introverts)

Table Talk: Total 22 (7 extroverts and 15 introverts)

When given time to think and respond and the structure for interaction, introverts do like to cooperate and learn with others.

Presenter Talk: Total: 2 (2 extroverts and 0 introverts)

Significantly low number, a reminder that this method should be kept to a minimum. We may assume that by teaching the whole class and lecturing we are catering for the introvert. Sometimes when its a lecture and whole class discussion, the introvert is less likely to participate than in smaller safer groups.

Suggestion: *When planning values-based approaches, whilst valuing all methods, consider using more 'Table Talk'. This co-operative approach will help introverts to feel as much at home as extroverts and encourage them to talk more in a safer context.*

22. Leading with Quiet Power – The silent voice of the introvert in us all

Key Message: *Introverts and extroverts are strong leaders. Creating spaces for the quiet and not so quiet voices of all to be heard is a valuable component in all values-based schools.*

We all love silence for there is great power in the intro-version of quietness to help make sense of our world. We use silence to relax and think things over and, when we do, the silent voice of the unhurried mind can speak to us. This silent voice comes in many forms including feelings, emotions, imagination, creativity, insight or intuition. Each one of us is unique and in all schools, some students prefer to lead with quiet power by valuing quietness more than outer expression; and others prefer to value their outer expression more than quietness. Both personality traits are valuable and both forms of leadership are valued.

Introverts are strong leaders and have the ability to focus deeply and quietly on topics, creativity, activities and the 'whole picture'. They place careful value on the content and clarity of their answers and speak when they feel it is right. They have a particular talent for listening with empathy and patience.......and take time to respond to a question.

Extroverts are strong leaders and have the ability to appear 'bubbly', 'attractive' and can talk a lot. They have a talent to express an opinion quickly.......yet sometimes respond without careful thought or dominate a conversation. Whilst valuing their contributions, they need both nurturing and guidance to slow down, reflect more deeply on their creativity before responding and leave space for the silent one to speak.

Both introverts and extroverts need nurturing and guidance to understand and appreciate the personalities of others around them.

Suggestion: *Encourage the leadership of the quiet power in all students to be heard.*

23. Parenting

Key Message: *Parenting doesn't come with a handbook for each child. Every parent is unique each with their own personality and gifts.*

Parents are the child's first and foremost educators. The gift of parenting and parenting 'in loco parentis' carries many challenges for the self. They include:

i.   To know yourself – who you are.
ii. To make sense of the world in our own minds before sharing with our children.
iii. To appreciate that children are a reflection of the moral education they receive at home and from the example of others,
iv. To take time to listen and be a positive mirror for children.

When parents are asked: 'If, like a product, children come with a guarantee, what basic characteristics would they always possess?

The parents replied: Love, Peace, Respect, Goodness, Joy, and Happiness

Then asked: 'What has no expiry date in humans?' The

replies included laughter, love, and happiness.

Suggestion: Once in a while, invite parents into class to share in their children's learning – maybe read a story or two – or take their child to their workplace.

24. Assessment

Key Message: Nurture the value of soft skill indicators along the way and not just the end result

Subject-based assessment, in its many forms, has an important part to play. 'Hard' diagnostic, formative and summative evidence helps us to guide children to academic success. However, you cannot 'measure' values-based education though it is possible to consider indicators that inform and support the inner world of values. For example, UNESCO's Early Childhood Education website offers indicators for: 'Educating the Whole Child – social, spiritual, physical, intellectual, cultural and emotional dimensions', 'Valuing the unique combination of each and every child and each and every adult', and 'Keep the best interests of the child incorporated in all that we do', amongst many others.

Suggestion: Design your own collaboratively created 'in class' values-based indicators and enable the children to aim for and self assess their progress.

25. Mentoring and Peer Research

Key Message: *Keep learning and sharing with humility, love, and respect.*

Mentoring

Mentoring lifts learning and professionalism. It reduces stress caused by 'ticky box' judgment. It is active learning and review in constant progress with a trusted friend. It is natural leadership and self-leadership in action.

With a trusted colleague, consider:

a. What makes a good lesson?
b. What makes a good values-based lesson?
c. What can management do to help you achieve your goals?
d. Measure the success of the goals and report.
e. Ask what objectives are required to help lift the spirit and standard of learning.

Peer Research

Peer Research and the dissemination of findings and recommendations to others encourage the sharing of best practice and raising of standards. This form of appreciative inquiry links up two educators to view the best of a given 'single focus' practice in each other's classroom. Its effectiveness is measured by its simplicity, clarity, and transferability of good practice that is essential in the busy lives of teachers.

It empowers:

a. Task orientation to attain the best for all the students and the educator.
b. Trust between mentor and mentee.
c. Truth to recognize strengths and, with humility and in confidence, to recognize shortcomings on both sides.
d. Time to reflect on the task.
e. Teamwork to achieve well-being for all.
f. The re-affirmation that the aim of all learning is, firstly, education of the child and not just education of the subject.

Suggestion: Start small and keep it do-able and simple. For example: How do you do Peace Time?

26. Keeping your Heart and Mind open to Signposts, Possibilities, and Creativity

Key Message: Keep searching for new and wise ways of learning and teaching.

1. Keep your heart and mind open

Keeping your heart and mind open to signposts and possibilities inspires passion to continue to understand learning and life's mysteries. For example:

a. Research into DNA and how positive energy can make you 'glow'
b. Research into the resonance of consciousness especially the tonality of the voice.
c. Research into the Benefits of Positive Thinking
d. Be mindful that 5 minutes of positive thinking can boost positive energy for 5 hours whilst 5 minutes of negative energy can deplete energy for 5 hours.

Suggestion: Add current research and action research to your medium term teaching and learning strategies.

2. Simply Be Creative

Key Message: Be open to the brightness of creativity above the glass ceiling we sometimes place on ourselves and others.

Simply giving space to explore and be creative invites in

many possibilities. For example:

- Express how friendship is lived under the sea.
- Create a 'Kindness Club' with coupons of kindness to give away.
- Take part in World Values Day.
- Design a blanket of love then sleep on it.
- Invite grandparents to share 'The Good Old Days'
- Make a book of tender language
- Show understanding and compassion for all life forms and traditions.
- Involve the local community
- Create a Dream Board and an Action Board side by side.
- Choose your own.

Suggestion: *Create expressions of kindness, compassion, and creativity every day.*

27. Nurturing the Educator – Trust your Intuition

Key Message: *Look after your most precious gift – yourself.*

a. A Day at the Beach – a special moment

Imagine offering educators the opportunity to spend a day at the beachside to enjoy a day's training and some relaxation. Imagine now the theme: 'Discovering your Inner Beauty'. After the exploratory session, the staff was invited to walk alone on the beach or with a trusted friend

– to paddle in the warm water, make sculptures or write a value in the sand.

Now imagine the reality with educators from the school writing their favorite value on the sand. After 2 hours alone – they all chose the same value written in their own language. And the value? It was love.

Was this co-incidence or natural? Whatever the source, it was natural, heart-felt and left a deep impression.

Love attracts itself to its own attention and we are drawn to what we love. It was and still echoes as a powerful moment.

Outdoor Education is not just a subject but an avenue to explore the soul of the land and part of the spirit within ourselves.

Suggestion: *Take time out for you each day to 'connect' with nature.*

b. Bringing your own gifts and sharing them.

Key Message: *We are each unique with a gift that no-one else can give away.*

We each have a noble gift to bring to humanity. It could be a long-held dream, something original, something creative, something practical, a story or maybe something 'forgotten' until now. The secret of developing and nurturing your own gift is love – for in love there is no hardness, doubt or resistance – just a big heart. Sharing of gifts means that you are not defined by others but by yourself for your uniqueness and originality that dwells within the blueprint of your soul. The giving of your gift, in many ways, is a gift to yourself.

When the values-based atmosphere is right and your intuition is 'in tune' with your receptors – the possibilities emerge. There is space within each one of us that is waiting to be heard.

Suggestion: Trust your intuition.

28. Sustaining a Values-Based Approach to Learning

Key Message: *The loving presence of the educator who creates a values-based atmosphere, who models their values with kindness, and who nurtures the well-being, care and inspires high-quality learning for their children must first nurture and take care of themselves.*

Sustaining a values-based approach to learning can only succeed if we take care of ourselves as educators.

It is, therefore, essential that educators take time out to sustain themselves. Teaching is one of the most rewarding professions and also one of the most demanding. Opening and closing up to 7000 conversations in a day can be exhausting with a call for rest and quiet time a must for all. Educators are born givers who rarely ask for anything in return, yet, when did you last book an appointment with yourself. Time for oneself is essential to remember to be a 'human being', who you are, and not just a 'human doing' in your professional role.

Sustaining oneself as an educator means to nurture yourself by creating spaces every day to rejuvenate and re-generate your inner battery. If not, burn out can follow and the loving presence in the classroom will lower.

Consider the following to help heal the busy mind and tired body:

• In silence, make a date with yourself. It could be with a warm drink, sitting alone, playing your favorite music, being with friends and/or simply reflecting on one or more of your many qualities.
• Take time to do what you like doing.
• Take up a sport or recreational activity and keep to it.
• Step away from your professional role. Remember, your role is your role and not you the soul.
• Hold on to the best moments. You may never know how much you are helping someone.
• Get organized. Get rid of useless things that clutter your life. Educators are great 'hoarders'. Do you really need that poster from 20 years ago?
• Remember, no-one can take away your inner joy unless you let them.

- Feel grateful and show it. Express gratitude and kindness. It will come back to you, and that includes looking after your physical, emotional and spiritual health.

There are many approaches to looking after yourself without hurt or harm to yourself and others. Sustaining a values-based approach starts and ends with ourselves and how we navigate life and ourselves. Each person will find their own way.

Remember, too, the curriculum and all the nuts and bolts that go with it are there to guide and fit the child and not the child to be fitted to the curriculum. Beware falling into the trap of a world full of targets where we can stress out, forget the child in us all and the natural gifts we are born with to share and to give away with our vision, our voice and our values.

Suggestion: *Look after yourself as an educator. Follow your heart and nurture the hearts of others.*

29. Simple Things mean a lot – The Smiling Eyes activity

Key Message: *Little things mean so much and add to the energy and the atmosphere of a values-based school.*

We all do it. Remember birthdays, make someone or offer someone a cup of their favorite drink, ask about family and friends and genuinely listen to their stories. It's what helps to make the world go round wherever we are living and working, whatever our role and whatever circumstance we find ourselves in. We each have our own repertoire of 'little things we do' to help others and to raise their spirit whatever their role in the school. This form of warm-heartedness is a living energy that adds to a sense of belonging and purpose.

The 'Picture Frame Smiling Eyes Activity'.

Adding to the warm-heartedness and atmosphere of a values-based school is the 'Smiling Eyes Activity'.

Sit in a group with 5 to 6 colleagues. Then, one person holds an empty picture frame in their hand and lifts it so that they see their colleague's face through the frame. Smiles begin to grow around the group as eye to eye contact is made. Then, say something that you think your colleague would like to hear. Watch the eyes start to smile. The next step is to pass the picture frame around the group until everyone receives a message from the person next to them. The energy will continue to rise, eyes will smile and the glow will become brighter.

Once everyone has received a message, invite everyone to write on a 'post-it' note the one word that describes the energy they are feeling. The 'post-it' notes then go onto a cloud shape poster to represent the atmosphere that has been created with smiling eyes.

This activity mirrors the atmosphere we create in the classroom. The activity is also very successful with students of all ages.

Little things mean so much and often a little token of appreciation and gentle re-affirmation of our worth helps to keep the spirit bright and the teaching vocation a joy. Loving educators don't seek appreciation though it is always warmly received.

Suggestion: *Keep giving the simple things in life away. They mean so much to so many and will bring happiness to the hearts of all.*

30. Nurturing, Valuing and Knowing Ourselves

Key Message: *Love yourself. Be Kind to yourself. Take Care of yourself.*

It was Aristotle who stated:

'Knowing yourself is the beginning of all wisdom'.

It was Democritus who stated:

'The world is a theatrical stage and life is a rite of passage through it'.

Perhaps remembering and knowing who we are with a gift to give and role to play is the first step.

It's called nurturing the natural nature of ourselves – and to take care of our most precious gift – ourselves, our character, our values and our chosen destiny – with love.

Suggestion: *Choose a value or set of values that are close to your heart. Give yourself a positive affirmation each day. Live your life by those values and be the model.*

End Piece

Giving a Voice to All and Creating Partnerships

Every individual has much to share wherever they are in our one world. The school population of 600+ represents 30+ nationalities who speak with one language – the language of values. All regions of the world, and in this context, the Arab world has much wisdom, stories and secrets to share with the wider world. Partnerships with like-minded groups both in Kuwait and around the world who are in tune with their hearts and values-based education are proving to be a way forward. Through partnerships and understanding, we re-affirm that the key skills of listening, sharing, acceptance, tolerance and simply 'doing what is right' are becoming more and more essential.

At the Kuwait American School, in a world that is often too dominated by the external show and excessive social media, the students are learning about 'Quiet Power', the importance of stillness, creativity out of silence and the value of being a 'human being'.

As the journey continues - we have much to learn - about ourselves.

Appreciation for Living Values Education

The school is very grateful to the Living Values Education program for its vision, clarity, guidance, and practicalities. It's a great invitational model to explore, experience and express. Living Values Education invites in learning without borders and learning from the heart. The school is a safe place to learn and to be; and will, for sure, continue to grow from the root.

The Last Words from a student

Many of the graduating students from Grade 12 who have benefited from the school's Living Values Education program from their early childhood days to young maturity – are now entering the world as global citizens.

Rawan Koujah speaks on their behalf during her High Honors Graduation acceptance speech. Rawan is now studying Medicine at the University of Dublin.

An excerpt from her Acceptance Speech

With doors opening of various beginnings - rich with fascinating opportunities - we are gathered here to celebrate the end of one chapter and the beginning of a new one with pure independence, responsibility, and courage.

Our school has the dream of influencing and awakening the utmost capabilities of a person's positive powers and to educate and enlighten its students and staff through its core base: living values. The vision is to graduate you all - not only with high academic knowledge - but of high moral standards that depend on a person's ethics, values, goodness, and attitude towards life itself.

For us all, the process was not easy to carry out. Expecting responses to these teachings required patience and a strong source of belief. Sometimes we did not understand for in the end we are human.

As time went by, we began to unravel the secrets behind such values: respect, tolerance, honesty, and other values. The walls around us were disassembling - slowly fading away - creating a family of our own; a family of students and teachers. What others called school, we called family. And travelling deep into the family, lied our class; a family within a family.

Many of you may ponder as to what makes our bond so special? No, our relationships were not flawless. As a class, we had our ups and downs. However, with faith and determination, and acceptance, we managed to overcome various obstacles. When our paths seemed to diverge, the paths always managed to meet again. We traveled together, as a pack, never leaving a person behind, constantly encouraging the next step to be taken. When others feared, the rest would assure. When some fell, the rest lifted. Together we grew. Together we flourished. We saw through the flaws of each and every classmate and discovered the beauty within. We had many unforgettable moments.

However, now ends this phase and begins a journey to test our endurance and individuality. A journey built on the foundation of our childhood, our values and time together. Now, we stand before various paths, at the end of an intersection. Soon we will part our ways, choosing the path which suits our individual interest. However, none will be forgotten, for each one us here will travel, holding onto a piece of the soul of the others.

The Kuwait American School Policy
on Living Values Education

Overview

The Kuwait American School is a caring, values-based school committed to delivering international education to the highest academic standards. We educate the whole person towards the highest level of human consciousness in a learning environment of intercultural understanding and respect. Our mission is to serve our one world community by empowering valuable members of society.

Aim

At the Kuwait American School our aim is to underpin all that we do with values education.

What are Values?

• Values are the worthwhile qualities deep within each person that are shared through their presence, words, actions and character.
• Values guide our thinking and behavior.
• Many values are shared values which carry different meanings according to culture, context and individual experience.
• Sharing and living our values adds to the quality of living and learning for all.

The Living Values Aide Memoire

The Living Values Education Aide Memoire summarizes the 5 key components of Living Values Education:
- creating the atmosphere
- the heart of Living Values
- practicalities
- reaching out
- nurturing the soul

Aide Memoire attached

Creating a values-based atmosphere is an essential part of Living Values Education.

What are the 12 core values of Living Values Education?

The 12 core values are:
- peace
- respect
- love
- happiness
- freedom
- honesty
- humility
- tolerance
- cooperation
- responsibility
- simplicity
- unity

The list is not exclusive as additional values are welcomed.

How are the values addressed?

Each value is addressed on a monthly basis throughout the year either as:
- a single, separate value;
- as part of a complementary set of values - such as Peace and Self Respect; or
- in a living context.

Placing values in the context

Each school year, values are placed in a living context on a monthly basis as per the school calendar.

For example: one year, the themes were:
September – Peace
October – Self Respect
November – Honesty
December – Simplicity
January – Responsibility
February – Love
March – Cooperation
April – Happiness
May – Time for Me

Additional themes include: caring, kindness, thankfulness, courage, one world.

The 9 varieties of Living Values Education activities

The nine varieties of Living Values Education are as follows:

- reflection points
- imagining
- relaxation/ focusing exercises
- artistic expression
- self-development activities
- stories and activities that enhance Social Justice
- techniques for developing Social Cohesion
- applying curriculum knowledge and our shared values in everyday life
- self-generated activities

The place of Peace Time

Peace Time invites everyone to be still and quiet. Peacetime focuses on the self by using a variety of approaches:

- sitting quietly
- closing your eyes
- the playing of soft music
- the playing of background music whilst working
- a commentary that invites reflective thoughts
- a commentary that invites words of affirmation
- time to reflect on what has been learned
- time to be quietly creative

Training for Values

- Values cannot be taught; they can only be caught.
- Whilst the methodology and materials are shared and explained, it is the modeling of the values by the educator that makes all the difference.
- The school, therefore, places great significance on modeling the values at all levels.

Creating a family where values can be lived together

Positive atmospheres create the all-important element of how to live together — with a relational trust — based on 5 staff-generated indicators:

- a place where you are welcomed
- a place to feel at ease with yourself
- a place to know yourself
- a place to feel part of a team
- a place to feel loved, valued, respected, understood and safe

Positive atmospheres create settings that encourage

- the use of a shared language of values
- ethical behavior
- values-based leadership at all levels of responsibility
- a community of learning and giving that reaches out to others
- visual evidence of living our values

The place of assemblies

The value or theme for the month is introduced in the assembly at the start of the month.

Assemblies:

- invite in a quiet time for all students and staff to feel part of the KAS family
- create a central focus to encourage students to think about the theme
- offer high-quality stories, songs and/or presentations
- provide a place to model our values.

Assemblies for KG and Elementary Students

- Assemblies take place for KG and Elementary students three times a week and are led by students and staff. The content of the invitational assembly includes songs, movement, plays, public speaking, celebrations of class work, and reflection time.

Assemblies for Middle and High School Students

- Extended assemblies take place for Middle/ High students once or twice a month and are led by students and staff. The content of the invitational assemblies includes group workshops on a given theme, fundraising programs, plays, ethical issues of the day, and celebration of learning.
- Parents are regularly invited to attend assemblies.

What are the indicators for living in our values?

Student and staff needs

- to feel LVRUS – loved, valued, respected, understood and safe
- to have and to develop relationships and to learn to live together
- to develop a self-awareness and knowledge of the world outside of themselves
- to enjoy creative experiences, including internal reflection and outside exploration

Teaching and learning about values

- Teachers begin by explaining the meaning of the value.
- Students reflect on the value and what it means to them and their own behavior.
- Students use the value to guide their own actions.

Staff modeling

- using a range of voice tonalities
- valuing all students
- focusing on and emphasize the positive
- disapproving of the inappropriate behavior – never the student
- making time for one another
- being mutually supportive
- sharing and appreciating the school's values with

parents and the wider community

Student skill indicators

- showing helpful politeness and good manners to everyone in the school.
- speaking politely to others
- listening carefully to and thinking about what others are saying
- demonstrating the ability to reflect
- demonstrating the ability to empathize and show tolerance
- being able to visualize and use imagination
- being able to be still
- being able to express feelings constructively
- developing positive attitudes to work and play
- accepting personal responsibility for actions
- caring and showing respect for one another and their property.

School indicators

- a welcoming place
- a calm working atmosphere
- positive regard for one another
- value/ theme for the month displayed around the school
- appropriate evidence of student's values-based learning in rooms and hallways
- to treat others as you would like to be treated yourself

Assessment

The emerging indicators are as follows:

- A warm welcome to school
- A calm, friendly and engaging classroom environment
- Positive behavior of students that is consistently
  well managed
- An excellent attitude to work in lessons and respect
  for all in the learning environment
- Well planned programs for students to understand
  the importance of values in their lives and how to
  make their own ethical choices
- Positive student relationships in and out
  of the classroom
- Displayed evidence of values-based themes
  and learning
- Monitoring the atmosphere, engagement approaches
  and 'the way' learning is shared
- Anecdotal data through conversation and informal
  observation
- Formal observation of teaching and learning
- Tracking student academic achievement over time.

Key References

Living Values Activities for Children Book Series – 2000 to 2018

Learning: The Treasure Within – Report to UNESCO for the International Commission on Education for the Twenty-First Century – UNESCO -1996

UNESCO – Early Childhood Indicators - 2001

Quiet Power - Susan Cain - 2016

Nurturing the Intuitive Heart of Values-Based Education with Ancient Wisdom for Modern Times – Williams - 2017

Website Addresses

Living Values Education website - www.livingvalues.net
Kuwait American School - www.kas.edu.kw

Special Thanks

All the students, staff and parents at the Kuwait American School together with the core group of KAS Living Values Trainers and Facilitators: Batool Arjomand, Dina Eidan, Rita Kirhady, Hilton Lyners and Ioanna Vasileiadou

All of my dear friends and family for everyday inspiration. Angeliki Palatzidi for proof reading and context. The wisdom of the ancients.

Contact
Peter Williams – peter.williams@livingvalues.net

Living Values Education:
The Authentic Approach of the Facilitator
Aide Memoire

	The Message we give is through..	Walking the Talk	Everyone's Contribution is Valuable	Values
Creating a Welcoming Atmosphere	our face, our smile, our voice, our authenticity our approach.	... everyone feels Loved, Valued, Respected, Understood and Safe	Honoring all cultures, inviting their stories	Belonging Caring Empathy Sharing Add your own
	Reflection	Visualisation	Creative Expression	Values
The Heart of Living Our Values	"Whose values?" Our shared values - based on personal and cultural experiences	... the school / workplace of your dreams ... the world through the eyes of a child	... through art, mime, dance, music, games.	Creativity Joy Positivity Add your own
	LVE Theoretical Model	Exploring Experiencing Expressing	Examples of good practice	Values
Practicalities	Building positive behavior through active listening, conflict resolution, values-based discipline	Making use of LVE activities to focus on key values	Assemblies, videos, stories from around the world Learning from evaluation	Appreciation Professionalism Preparation Enthusiasm Add your own
	Action Planning	Creating tools and templates	Connecting locally and globally	Values
Reaching Out	Bringing values to life in a practical way including school / workplace / local community / environment	Locally and internationally generated resources	The International Dimension Social networks, e.g. LinkedIn	Innovation Sustaining Cooperation Adventure Generosity Add your own
	The Language of Silence	Sustaining ourselves as educators	Common Inheritance	Values
Nurturing the Soul	Reflection, taking time in nature	Create a personal 'tool kit'	Inter - connectedness	Peace Happiness Freedom Add your own